ADAPTED TO SURVIVE

ANIMALS THAT HUNT

Angela Royston

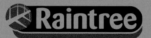

Raintree is an imprint of Capstone Global Library Limited, a company incorporated in England and Wales having its registered office at 7 Pilgrim Street, London, EC4V 6LB – Registered company number: 6695582

www.raintreepublishers.co.uk
myorders@raintreepublishers.co.uk

Edited by Dan Nunn, Rebecca Rissman, and Helen Cox Cannons
Designed by Joanna Hinton-Malivoire
Picture research by Mica Brancic
Originated by Capstone Global Library Ltd
Production by Helen McCreath
Printed and bound in China

ISBN 978 1 406 27088 4
17 16 15 14 13
10 9 8 7 6 5 4 3 2 1

British Library Cataloguing in Publication Data
A full catalogue record for this book is available from the British Library.

Acknowledgements
We would like to thank the following for permission to reproduce photographs: Corbis p. 19 (National Geographic Society/© Ralph Lee Hopkins); Getty Images p. 7 (National Geographic/Jim and Jamie Dutcher); Naturepl.com pp. 4 (© Mary McDonald), 10 (© Anup Shah), 12 (© Andy Rouse), 13 (© Steven Kazlowski), 15, 24, 29 bottom right (© Pete Oxford), 16 (© Edwin Giesbers), 18 (© Brandon Cole), 21, 29 bottom left (© Eric Baccega), 23 (© Alex Hyde), 25 (© Sue Daly), 26, 27 (© Ingo Arndt); Shutterstock pp. 29 top left (© Volodymyr Burdiak), 29 top right (© Critterbiz); SuperStock pp. 5 (Biosphoto), 6 (Universal Images Group), 8 (imagebroker.net), 9 (age fotostock), 11, 14 (Minden Pictures), 17 (Angelo Cavalli), 20 (Juniors), 22 (age fotostock).

Cover photograph of a mountain lion (*Felis concolor*) captive in winter habitat reproduced with permission of Getty Images (All Canada Photos/Don Johnston).

We would like to thank Michael Bright for his invaluable help in the preparation of this book.

Every effort has been made to contact copyright holders of material reproduced in this book. Any omissions will be rectified in subsequent printings if notice is given to the publisher.

Some words are shown in bold, **like this**. You can find out what they mean by looking in the glossary.

CONTENTS

GOOD AT HUNTING

Hunters are animals that attack and kill other animals for food. They are called **predators** and they include large animals, such as tigers, and small animals, such as spiders. Predators are found nearly everywhere – wherever there are animals to feed on!

Predators can live in forests, deserts, grasslands, or in the sea. These Cape foxes are predators.

WHY DO ANIMALS HUNT?

Living things need food to give them energy. Plants make their own sugary food using the energy of sunlight. Animals cannot make their own food. Many animals, such as deer and mice, eat plants. However, some animals, such as cougars, have to eat meat.

These deer only eat grass and other plants.

cougar

Predators hunt
other animals in
order to **survive**.

DEADLY WEAPONS

Adaptations are special things about an animal's body that help it to **survive**. For example, **predators** have deadly weapons, such as sharp claws or **venomous** stings. Hunters also have particular skills that help them to find **prey**. They may be particularly good at seeing, smelling, or hearing.

sharp claws

Super hearing
A wolf can hear sounds up to 16 kilometres (10 miles) away!

LIONS

Lions are hunters, like all big cats. They move fast and have sharp teeth, which they use to kill **prey**. Lions hunt antelope and other plant-eating animals. They creep close to their prey and wait for the right moment to attack.

DID YOU KNOW?
Female lions hunt down prey, but they let the male lion eat first!

POLAR BEARS

Polar bears hunt for seals on the icy Arctic Ocean. The bears have sharp claws and teeth. They often wait by a hole in the ice for a seal to appear and then they pounce!

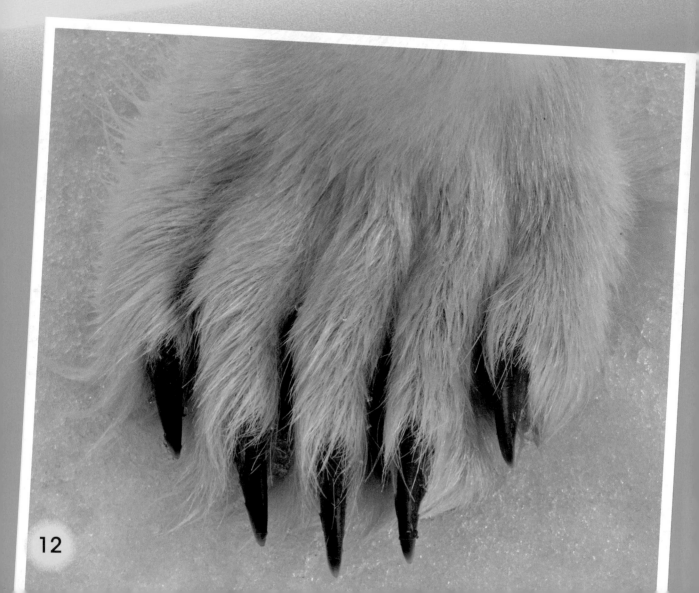

Largest predator

When an adult polar bear stands on its back legs to attack, it can be more than 3 metres (10 feet) tall!

SHARKS

Sharks have many **adaptations** for hunting. They swim fast and they have strong jaws and sharp teeth, which rip or crush their **prey**. Sharks have special senses that help them to find prey. They can even **detect** tiny movements in the water made by other animals.

DID YOU KNOW?
Sharks can smell the blood of an injured animal 500 metres (1,640 feet) away!

CROCODILES

Crocodiles are **reptiles** that live in rivers, lakes, and ponds. They are well **adapted** to hunting. They have powerful jaws and many sharp teeth. Each tooth has a new tooth growing inside it, ready to take over when the old tooth falls out.

nose

A crocodile lies in wait with only its eyes and nose above the water.

DID YOU KNOW?
A crocodile may go through 3,000 teeth during its life!

KILLER WHALES

Killer whales are the fiercest sea hunters. Their **streamlined** bodies cut through water, and their sharp teeth tear fish, squid, and other small **prey** before swallowing them whole. Killer whales sometimes hunt alone, but more often they gang up to attack much larger animals.

Groups of killer whales attack sharks and even large whales.

BIRDS OF PREY

Owls and other **birds of prey** grab their **prey** with their two strong legs and sharp claws, called talons. Birds of prey can spot a tiny mouse on the ground far below them. Their hooked beaks tear the meat apart.

talons

Fantastic eyesight
Birds of prey can see
8 to 10 times better
than humans can!

LONG TONGUES

Chameleons and frogs have an amazing **adaptation** for catching food. When an insect flies close, the chameleon or frog whips out its tongue and grabs it! A chameleon's tongue is longer than its body (not counting its tail).

Longest tongue
A chameleon's tongue can catch an insect up to 14 centimetres (5½ inches) away!

DEADLY POISONS

Many hunters use **venom** to kill **prey**. They include some snakes, spiders, and jellyfish. Snakes and spiders **inject** their venom through hollow fangs. Some box jellyfish are so **venomous** they can kill a person in less than 5 minutes.

fang

A jellyfish's **tentacles** are covered with venomous stings.

TRAPDOOR SPIDER

Spiders use **venom** to **paralyse** or kill their **prey**. To catch prey, a trapdoor spider digs a hole and spins a web to cover the opening. The spider hides in the hole and waits. When an insect touches the web, the spider pushes up the trapdoor, leaps out, and catches it.

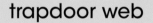

trapdoor web

trapdoor

ANIMAL CHALLENGE

1. Why would an elephant not make a good hunter?

2. What weapons did Tyrannosaurus rex have?

3. What **adaptations** do wolves have for hunting?

Invent your own hunting animal. Think about what animals it might feed on and what weapons it would need. You can use some of the adaptations in the photos, or make up your own.

sharp teeth

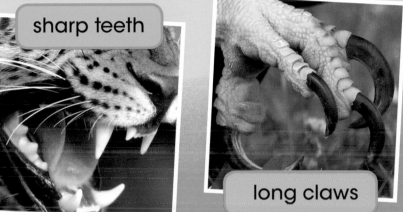

long claws

fangs

hooked beak

Answers to Animal Challenge

1. Elephants have tusks and are massively heavy. But they are too big to creep up on other animals!

2. Tyrannosaurus rex had sharp teeth and strong jaws.

3. As well as good hearing, wolves have sharp teeth. They often hunt in groups, called packs.

GLOSSARY

adaptation special thing about an animal's body that helps it to survive in a particular way or in a particular place

adapted well suited to a particular activity or way of living

bird of prey bird that hunts and eats small animals, such as mice and other birds

detect discover or notice

inject to force a liquid into the body

paralyse to make something unable to move

predator animal that hunts and kills other animals for food

prey animal that is hunted and eaten by another animal

reptile animal that is covered with scales and lays eggs

streamlined smooth, pointed shape that moves through air or water easily

survive manage to go on living

tentacles long feelers that some sea animals use to move and to attack other animals

venom liquid poison that is injected into prey

venomous poisonous

FIND OUT MORE

BOOKS

Deadliest Animals, Melissa Stewart (National Geographic, 2011)

Deadly Predators (Animal Attack), Camilla de la Bédoyère (QED, 2012)

Polar Bear vs Seal, Mary Meinking (Raintree, 2011)

WEBSITES

kids.nationalgeographic.co.uk/kids/animals/creaturefeature
Click on particular animals, such as great white sharks, lions, or Nile crocodiles, to find out more about them.

www.bbc.co.uk/nature/adaptations/Predation
This BBC website includes short videos showing how several different animals hunt.

www.ypte.org.uk/animal-facts.php
Find out more about many different animals on this website.

INDEX